NEW ZEALAND

Frogs &
Reptiles

Brian Gill
Curator of Land Vertebrates, Auckland Museum
and
Tony Whitaker

David Bateman

Produced with the assistance of the New Zealand Lottery Grants Board.

NEW ZEALAND
Lottery Grants Board
TE POARI ROTA

Published in 1996 by David Bateman Limited,
Tarndale Grove, Albany Business Park, Bush Road,
Albany, Auckland, New Zealand

Reprinted 1998

Design by Shelley Watson
Printed in Hong Kong by Colorcraft Limited

Contents

Introduction

New Zealand is the most isolated land-mass of its size and few types of amphibians and reptiles have reached its shores. The only groups occurring naturally in New Zealand are frogs, tuataras, two families of lizards (geckos and skinks), sea-snakes and marine turtles – see Table 1 (page 6). Salamanders, toads, land snakes, tortoises and terrapins (freshwater turtles) are absent. The tuataras (*Sphenodon*) and native frogs (*Leiopelma*) are archaic animals of exceptional scientific interest and, with other oddities like the kiwis, they ensure New Zealand's place in zoological textbooks.

The ancestors of the tuataras and native frogs probably walked here about 160–200 million years ago when the area we now know as New Zealand was joined to other southern land-masses to form the super-continent Gondwanaland.

Geckos and skinks are renowned for their powers of dispersal and are widely distributed throughout the Pacific. It was earlier believed that adult geckos and skinks, or their eggs, arrived on driftwood after New Zealand became an island. However, recent studies of the biochemical genetics of the New Zealand species suggest that they have been isolated much longer than had been previously thought, and they too may have reached New Zealand by land before its separation from Gondwanaland about 85 million years ago.

This book deals with the 59 living species of frogs and reptiles reported wild in New Zealand – six frogs, two tuataras, 16 geckos, 28 skinks, five marine turtles and two sea-snakes. Axolotls (larvae of the salamander *Ambystoma mexicanum*) and several species of terrapins and tortoises are kept in captivity in New Zealand but have not naturalised in the wild

Table 1. Classification of the 15 genera and 9 families of New Zealand amphibians and reptiles.
An asterisk (*) indicates an introduced genus.

CLASS	ORDER	FAMILY	GENUS
Amphibia (Amphibians)	Anura (Frogs & toads)	Leiopelmatidae	*Leiopelma*
		Hylidae	**Litoria*
Reptilia (Reptiles)	Testudines (Tortoises, terrapins & turtles	Cheloniidae	*Caretta, Chelonia, Eretmochelys, Lepidochelys*
		Dermochelyidae	*Dermochelys*
	Sphenodontida (Tuataras & extinct allies)	Sphenodontidae	*Sphenodon*
	Squamata (Lizards & snakes)	Gekkonidae	*Hoplodactylus, Naultinus*
		Scincidae	*Cyclodina, *Lampropholis, Oligosoma*
		Hydrophiidae	*Pelamis*
		Laticaudidae	*Laticauda*

and are not included here. The North Island has a greater diversity of wild species than the rest of New Zealand, and one group – the *Cyclodina* skinks – is restricted to the North Island.

The exact number of lizards in New Zealand is not yet decided and is likely to increase as more research is done. The biochemical genetics of the native lizards is currently the subject of much study which suggests that many of the more variable lizards comprise several 'cryptic' species that have not been previously recognised. Several new species are likely to be described in the near future, but for the purposes of this guide we can merely note in some of the species accounts the likelihood of this happening.

The aim of this book is to enable identification of New Zealand's frogs and reptiles. Six 'keys' are provided to show how to differentiate between the species. The keys contain pairs of mutually exclusive statements in a numbered sequence, and only one of the statements should apply to the specimen whose identity is sought. Each statement ends with the identity of the specimen or the number of the next couplet to be consulted. Starting at 1, follow the prescribed sequence of couplets until you reach an identity. A magnifying glass will be helpful for certain diagnostic features on the head and feet of geckos and skinks.

No key is perfect and an imperfect key is better than none at all. Problems with the present keys are acknowledged, particularly the use of distribution and maximum size as 'distinguishing' characters and the failure to separate some species of small brown skinks whose diagnostic features cannot be set down simply, if at all. Note also that colour and colour-pattern can be extremely variable in New Zealand lizards, making identification difficult on these characteristics alone. Only limited success can be expected in attempting to identify juvenile lizards, as their colour-pattern is often much less distinct than in adults.

The keys do not cover eggs, which are produced by the frogs, the tuataras and two skinks. Turtles and some sea-snakes lay eggs, but none of the marine reptiles breed in New Zealand. Tadpoles are not included in the key to frogs.

The most useful measurement of the size of most frogs and reptiles is the length from

snout to vent (SVL). This is measured along the belly from the tip of the snout to the end of the body in frogs, or to the vent – the slit at the base of the tail – in lizards and tuataras.

Having identified a specimen using the keys, check the illustration and notes for that species to see that they match. Any new or unusual records of frogs or reptiles should be reported to a major museum or to an officer of the Department of Conservation.

Tuataras have been protected by law since 1895 and the native frogs since 1922. More recent legislation protects the native lizards. New Zealand is a signatory to the Convention on International Trade in Endangered Species (CITES), which, for example, blocks the entry into New Zealand of products obtained from marine turtles.

KEY TO THE GROUPS OF FROGS AND REPTILES

1a	Skin scaly; long tail or carapace (shell) present .... (Reptiles) **2**	
1b	Skin not scaly; tail and carapace absent .... Frogs (p. 10)	
2a	Limbs present **3**	
2b	Limbs absent .... Sea-snakes (p. 93)	
3a	Carapace present; tail relatively short .... Turtles (p. 93)	
3b	Carapace absent; tail long... **4**	
4a	Prominent ridge running above each eye to snout; adults with crest along mid-line of back .... Tuataras (p. 22)	
4b	Not as above .... (Lizards) **5**	
5a	Skin soft, loose and matt; body scales granular; eyes large and unblinking (lower eyelid fixed as transparent spectacle) .... Geckos (p. 27)	
5b	Skin firm, tight and shiny; body scales flat; eyes small and blinking (lower eyelid moveable) .... Skinks (p. 53)	

Frogs

Frogs are the largest group of amphibians – the backboned animals with soft, moist, glandular skins. Typically they live in damp, marshy situations and lay unshelled eggs in water. The eggs hatch into swimming larvae (tadpoles) that breathe through gills and undergo a metamorphosis to become air-breathing terrestrial adults. This is so with the three Australian frogs (*Litoria*) introduced to New Zealand, but the three native species (*Leiopelma*) lay clusters of 4–19 large, yolky eggs (8–20 mm diameter) in damp, muddy sites under logs and stones. The tadpole stage occurs within the egg and it is a tailed froglet that hatches and later absorbs the tail.

The native frogs are of great scientific interest because they have various primitive anatomical features not found in other modern frogs. As they are small, secretive, silent (but for faint chirps) and restricted in habitat and distribution, they are far less likely to be seen than the introduced frogs which are common, brightly coloured, vocal and widespread in most areas of human settlement.

Frogs are carnivores, eating any moving prey (mainly arthropods such as insects and spiders) that they can over-power. The three introduced frogs have brightly coloured groins. This colour is exposed as the frog leaps forward and the legs trail behind, but it disappears when the frog comes to rest and the legs fold up. This is called 'flash coloration' and the flashing of this colour as the frog hops may confuse a predator.

KEY TO FROGS

1a   External eardrum absent; pupil more or less rounded; thighs drab; no loud breeding call .... (native frogs *Leiopelma*) **2**

1b   External eardrum discernible behind eye; pupil a horizontal slit; thighs brightly coloured; breeding call loud ....
.... (introduced frogs *Litoria*) **4**

2a   Webs on hind toes distinct; longitudinal ridge behind eye not distinct; body and limbs robust ....
.... Hochstetter's Frog *Leiopelma hochstetteri* (p. 14)

2b   Webs on hind toes absent or nearly so; longitudinal ridge behind eye distinct; body and limbs slender **3**

3a   Relatively small, up to 37 mm SVL; mainly green, mainly brown, or green and brown ....
.... Archey's Frog *Leiopelma archeyi* (p. 11)

3b   Relatively large, up to 49 mm SVL; brown, not conspicuously green except rarely in juveniles ....
.... Hamilton's Frog *Leiopelma hamiltoni* (p. 13)

4a   Skin changes colour between pale and dark brown; thighs orange; not larger than about 42 mm SVL; call cricket-like ....
....Whistling Frog *Litoria ewingii* (p. 17)

4b   Skin changes colour between green and blue-black; thighs blue; often exceeds 42 mm SVL; call a croak or drone **5**

5a   Back rather warty; pale stripe present along mid-line of back; toe pads no wider than toes; call a set of simple harsh croaks ..
.... Golden Bell Frog *Litoria raniformis* (p. 18)

5b   Back almost smooth; vertebral stripe absent; toe pads $1^1/_2$ times wider than toes; call a prolonged, descending, three-syllabled drone .... Green Frog *Litoria aurea* (p. 15)

Archey's Frog   *Leiopelma archeyi*

Archey's Frog
Leiopelma archeyi   Turbott, 1942

Description: Colour variable from mainly green (rarely) through combinations of green and brown to mainly brown. Thighs not brightly coloured. Build relatively slender. Hind toes not (or scarcely) webbed. A distinct glandular ridge runs backwards from the eye. No external eardrum.

Size: Males up to 31 mm SVL; females up to 37 mm SVL.

Hamilton's Frog   *Leiopelma hamiltoni*

Distribution: Moehau and Colville Ranges on the Coromandel Peninsula south to ranges near Paeroa. Whareorino Forest, west of Te Kuiti.

Habitat: Moist native forest, grassy clearings and sub-alpine scrub at 200–1,000 m altitude. Often occurs on mist-shrouded ridges away from creeks.

Habits: Terrestrial. Nocturnal. Shelters by day under stones and logs. No loud breeding call.

Notes: Named after Sir Gilbert Archey (1890–1974), former Director of the Auckland Institute and Museum. **Endangered.**

Hamilton's Frog
Leiopelma hamiltoni   McCulloch, 1919

Description: Mainly brown; juveniles occasionally greenish. Thighs not brightly coloured. Build relatively slender. Hind toes not (or scarcely) webbed. A distinct glandular ridge runs backwards from the eye. No external eardrum. Similar in appearance to *L. archeyi* (previous page) but larger on average.

Size: Males up to 43 mm SVL; females up to 49 mm SVL.

Distribution: Known only from Stephens and Maud Islands in the Marlborough Sounds area. Subfossil bones attributed to this species have been found in the Waitomo, Hawkes Bay, Wairarapa and north-west Nelson areas proving that the species was once more generally distributed.

Habitat: Coastal forest (Maud Island) and a deep boulder bank (Stephens Island).

Habits: Terrestrial with some ability to climb. Nocturnal. Shelters by day in damp crevices. No loud breeding call.

Notes: Named after Harold Hamilton who collected the first specimens discovered. One of the world's rarest amphibians; less than 200 on Stephens Island but perhaps nearly 20,000 on Maud. Biochemical studies have suggested that the population on Maud Island is genetically distinctive and it may be described as a new species in the near future. **Endangered.**

Hochstetter's Frog

Leiopelma hochstetteri Fitzinger, 1861

Description: Mainly brown; occasionally greenish. Thighs not brightly coloured. Stockily built with robust limbs. Forelimbs broader and more muscular in males. Hind toes webbed for about half their length. No external eardrum.

Size: Males up to 38 mm SVL; females up to 47 mm SVL.

Distribution: Northland south of Whangarei; Waitakere, Hunua and Rangitoto Ranges; Whareorino forest, west of Te Kuiti; Great Barrier Island; Coromandel Peninsula; Bay of Plenty; East Cape region. Subfossil bones attributed to this species have been found in the Waitomo, Hawkes Bay and north-west Nelson areas proving that the species was once even more generally distributed.

Habitat: Shaded creek edges in native forest up to about 800 m altitude.

Habits: Semi-aquatic. Nocturnal. Shelters by day in wet cavities and crevices beneath stones or logs, usually near shaded creeks. No loud breeding call.

Notes: The most widely distributed native frog and thus the one most often found. Very different in appearance and habitat from the other two species. Named after Dr Ferdinand von Hochstetter (1829–84), an Austrian geologist who travelled widely in New Zealand and took the first specimens of this frog to Europe. **Endangered.**

Hochstetter's Frog   *Leiopelma hochstetteri*

Green Frog
Litoria aurea   (Lesson, 1829)

Description: Similar in appearance to *L. raniformis* (p. 18) but golden markings are often less extensive and less broken up, stripe along mid-line of back is absent, back is smoother, and toe pads are $1^1/2$ times wider than toes.

Size: Up to about 85 mm SVL.

Distribution: Coastal New South Wales and eastern Victoria. In New Zealand (introduced) at present restricted to Northland, Auckland, Waikato, Coromandel Peninsula and Bay of Plenty.

Habitat: Farmed and settled areas and along bush edges, usually in or near swamps, lakes, large ponds and sluggish streams.

Habits: Not a strong climber. Nocturnal, or active by day in or near water. Calls in or near water. Call a drawn-out, descending, three-syllabled drone. May emit piercing shrieks when alarmed or distressed.

Green Frog   *Litoria aurea*

Notes: Introduced from Australia, probably in the 1860s. May spread to other areas naturally or with accidental or deliberate human assistance. The specific name means 'golden'. Known in Australia as the 'Green and Golden Bell Frog'. **Not protected.**

Whistling Frog
Litoria ewingii   (Duméril & Bibron, 1841)

Description: Brown; changes shade between pale and dark brown. Thighs orange. External eardrum discernible in dark brown band that extends behind eye.

Size: Males up to 37 mm SVL; females up to 47 mm SVL.

Distribution: South-east Australia, including Tasmania. In New Zealand (introduced), widespread in South and Stewart Islands. In North Island mainly in Manawatu area from Bulls to Otaki, but pockets occur elsewhere, e.g., Wanganui.

Habitat: Bush, farmland and urban areas. Has been recorded above the tree-line in the South Island.

Habits: Will climb several metres above ground. Largely nocturnal. Hides by day in vegetation or under logs and stones, often far from water. Calls at night (or on damp days) throughout the year. Call a set of 4–14 shrill, cricket-like 'creee' sounds, the first prolonged. Spawns April-December (Manawatu) or all year (Westland). Bunches of spawn are wound around submerged stems and stalks. Tadpoles may be found in any month and reach 50 mm total length. Often breeds in ephemeral pools and puddles, frequently far from permanent water.

Whistling Frog   *Litoria ewingii*

Notes: Introduced from Tasmania to Greymouth in 1875 and from the South Island to the Manawatu in about 1948. Likely to spread throughout the country in time. Known in Australia as the 'Brown Tree Frog'. **Not protected.**

Golden Bell Frog
Litoria raniformis   (Keferstein, 1867)

Description: Bright green with golden markings. The green can darken to blue-black. A distinct cream-coloured fold runs backwards from the eye. Mid-line of back has a pale stripe. Back warty. Thighs bright blue. Toe pads not wider than toes. External eardrum obvious behind eye.

Size: Males up to 65 mm SVL; females up to 92 mm SVL.

Distribution: South-east Australia, including Tasmania. Widespread in New Zealand (introduced).

Habitat: As for *L. aurea* (p. 15).

Habits: Call a series of harsh croaks. Other habits as for *L. aurea* (p. 15). Starts spawning in September. The bunches of spawn may sink or float but are not usually attached to anything. Tadpoles may reach 100 mm (rarely 150 mm) total length.

Golden Bell Frog *Litoria raniformis*

Notes: Introduced from Australia. The first known release was in 1867. The specific name means 'Rana-like', *Rana* being the genus to which the 'typical' frogs of Europe belong. **Not protected.**

Tuataras

The lizard-like tuataras, unique to New Zealand, have achieved world-wide fame among zoologists as the only surviving representatives of the Order Sphenodontida, one of the four groups into which the living reptiles of the world are divided. Their relatives died out elsewhere in the world at least 60 million years ago. The tuataras are among the most primitive of living reptiles, having undergone few evolutionary changes in anatomy during the past 200 million years. They are often referred to as 'living fossils'.

Tuataras can shed and regrow their tail as lizards do. Tuatara is a Maori name meaning 'peaks on the back', a reference to the dorsal spines.

Copulation occurs in late summer or autumn, and eggs are laid in early summer following. Clutches of 8–19 eggs (average of 10) are laid in holes in the ground and covered. Eggs are about 30 mm long with tough, white, leathery shells. The incubation period is 11–16 months. Tuataras reach sexual maturity after about 13 years and can live at least 60 years. Females reproduce on average only once every four years. Tuataras have a loud croaking call.

1a   Dorsal surfaces dark olive-green; North Brother Island only .....
          .... Günther's Tuatara *Sphenodon guntheri* (p. 22)
1b   Dorsal surfaces pale olive-green or slate-grey; not North
          Brother Island .... Tuatara *Sphenodon punctatus* (p. 23)

Günther's Tuatara
Sphenodon guntheri   Buller, 1877

Description: Dorsal surfaces dark olive-green. Otherwise, as
for Tuatara (p. 23).

Size: Up to 250 mm SVL, and up to 660 g in weight. Males
larger than females.

Distribution: Known only from North Brother Island (of The
Brothers group), Cook Strait.

Habitat: Low growths of shrubs including taupata and *Hebe*.

Habits: Presumed to be largely as for Tuatara (p. 23).

Notes: Named after Albert Günther (1830–1914), Keeper of
Reptiles at the British Museum, London, 1856–95, who first
recognised that tuataras belong in an order of their own.
Wild population estimated to be about 300. **Endangered.**

Günther's Tuatara   *Sphenodon guntheri*

Tuatara
Sphenodon punctatus   (Gray, 1842)

Description: Olive-green or slate-grey; finely speckled. Lizard-like, but differs from New Zealand lizards in having a wedge-shaped head with a prominent ridge running above each eye to the snout. Adults have a crest of soft spines along the mid-line of the head and body. The crest is more strongly developed in males and is raised during courtship displays. A toothed ridge runs along the upper mid-line of the tail. No external earhole.

Size: Males may reach 280 mm SVL (610 mm total length) and weigh up to 1.3 kg. Females are smaller and rarely exceed 500 g.

Distribution: Formerly widespread throughout New Zealand (as indicated by the occurrence of subfossil bones). Now restricted to about 30 offshore islands in the Marlborough Sounds area and along the east coast of the North Island from Northland to Bay of Plenty.

Habitat: Coastal forest and clearings, especially where the ground has been tunnelled by nesting seabirds.

Habits: Nocturnal, but often sun-basks. Carnivorous, feeding on arthropods, lizards, and seabird eggs and chicks.

Notes: The specific name means 'spotted'. The population on Little Barrier Island, of which few individuals have been found, has been named as a separate subspecies (*S. p. reischeki*).

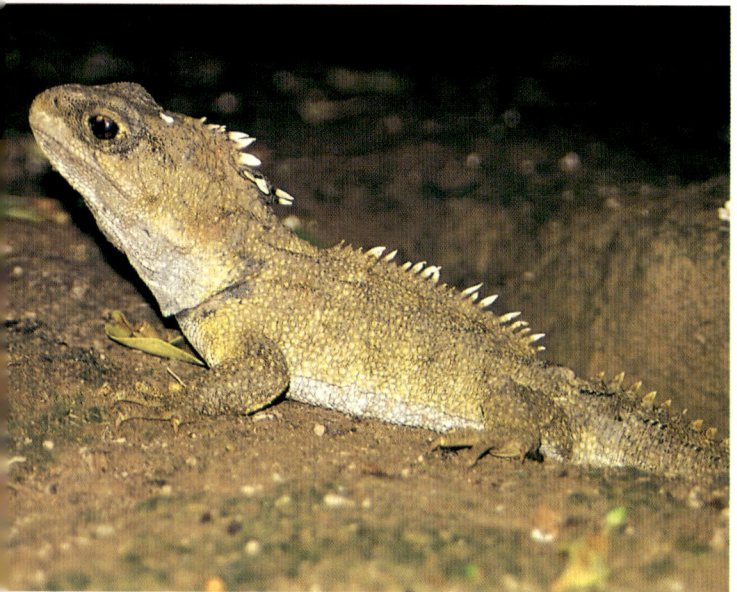

Tuatara   *Sphenodon punctatus*

Geckos

The geckos are a large family of lizards common throughout the warmer regions of the world. Geckos have large eyes covered by transparent scales that are shed along with the skin. In the course of evolution, the lower eyelid has fused shut, but one transparent scale on it has enlarged to cover the eye. Since the eyelids do not move, geckos cannot blink. If the eyes are dirty, the gecko licks them clean with its large fleshy tongue.

The body scales are small and granular giving the skin a dull, velvety appearance. The skin is shed whole or in large pieces.

Mature male geckos have a swelling at the base of their tail to accommodate the paired sex organs (hemipenes). All the geckos of the world lay eggs except the New Zealand species (and at least one species from New Caledonia) which give birth to live young, usually twins.

Most reptiles are silent but geckos are an exception. The New Zealand geckos have chirping or chattering communication calls; in addition, the green geckos make a loud croak of alarm or distress, and the *Hoplodactylus* geckos have a shrill squeal.

The New Zealand geckos fall into two groups. The grey-brown geckos (*Hoplodactylus*) are rather drab and come out at night (some species sun-bask readily and *H. granulatus* and *H. rakiurae* are at least partly diurnal). They have wide pads on the undersurfaces of their toes which assist in climbing smooth vertical obstacles. The intensity of the skin colour can change between pale and dark.

The green geckos (*Naultinus*) are active by day and have

slender toes well adapted for grasping twigs and climbing among foliage. They cannot alter their skin colour. All New Zealand geckos will shed their tails to escape from predators, but the green geckos are less disposed to do so because they use the tail for grasping as they climb. They can hang by the tail if necessary.

New Zealand geckos are omnivores, eating mainly arthropods such as insects and spiders, but seasonally taking significant quantities of soft fruits and some nectar from flowers. Some species also eat carrion, such as regurgitated food from seabirds.

KEY TO GECKOS

1a   Bright green (rarely bright yellow) or, if dull green and brown, the overall pattern is not herring-boned (some males from Canterbury are brown, grey and white without green); mouth lining blue or purple; scales on flat upper surface of snout noticeably larger than body scales; some scales on back or flanks may be enlarged (in South Island only); toes narrow, tapering; enlarged lamellae under toes in continuous series from sole to claw; tail thin, able to grip well; active by day ......
.... (green geckos *Naultinus*) **2**

1b   Dull grey-brown, or pale yellow-green or, if dull green and brown, the overall pattern is distinctly herring-boned; mouth lining pink or orange; scales on flat upper surface of snout not noticeably larger than body scales; back and flank scales never enlarged; toes generally expanded to wide pads; lamellae under toes in broken series (except *H. granulatus, H. nebulosus, H. kahutarae* and *H. rakiurae*); tail thick, unable to grip well; mainly active at night ....
.... (grey-brown geckos *Hoplodactylus*) **8**

2a   North Island only **3**

2b   South and Stewart Islands only **4**

3a   Tongue blue; scales of snout dome-shaped; 3 or more post-mental scales (the row of small scales immediately behind the enlarged scale at the tip of the 'chin') ....
.... Common Green Gecko *Naultinus elegans* (p. 43)

3b   Tongue red; scales of snout flat; usually 2 post-mentals ....
.... Northland Green Gecko *Naultinus grayii* (p. 46)

4a   Enlarged scales on body and head **5**

4b   Enlarged scales only on head and nape **6**

5a   Enlarged conical scales over entire body ....
.... Rough Gecko *Naultinus rudis* (p. 48)

5b   Enlarged scales only on head and in a line along sides (only nape and lower back in Stephens Island specimens) ....
.... Marlborough Green Gecko *Naultinus manukanus* (p. 47)

6a	Scales of body generally conical or rounded .... West Coast Green Gecko *Naultinus tuberculatus* (p. 50)
6b	Scales of body generally granular 7
7a	Row of scales immediately above eyes conical .... Jewelled Gecko *Naultinus gemmeus* (p. 45)
7b	Row of scales immediately above eyes rounded .... Nelson Green Gecko *Naultinus stellatus* (p. 49)
8a	Back brown, dark green (or olive) and white in a distinctive herring-boned pattern; mouth lining pinkish grey; Stewart Island only .... Harlequin Gecko *Hoplodactylus rakiurae* (p. 41)
8b	No dark green patches or herring-boned pattern on back; mouth lining not pinkish grey; not restricted to Stewart Island **9**
9a	Back distinctly striped, with no large irregular patches, and 2 stripes come together abruptly at the tail **10**
9b	Back banded or with large irregular patches (or, if striped, there are patches as well and 2 stripes rarely come together abruptly at the tail) **11**
10a	Rostral (single large scale at very tip of snout) extends to nostrils (Fig. 1); males with 3 enlarged pointed scales on each side at base of tail .... Striped Gecko *Hoplodactylus stephensi* (p. 42)
10b	Rostral not in contact with nostrils (Fig. 2); males with 1 enlarged blunt scale on each side at base of tail .... Goldstripe Gecko *Hoplodactylus chrysosireticus* (p. 31)
11a	Light stripe connects eye and ear on each side; much white on 'lips'; V-shaped mark on head between eyes; mouth lining orange or yellow **12**
11b	Band connecting eye and ear dull or absent; 'lips' not brightly speckled with white; V-shaped mark on head between eyes usually absent; mouth lining pink **13**
12a	Snout rather pointed; undersurfaces heavily blotched; not Stewart Island .... Forest Gecko *Hoplodactylus granulatus* (p. 34)

Figure 1 Tip of the snout of a gecko showing rostral scale (R) in contact with nostrils (N)

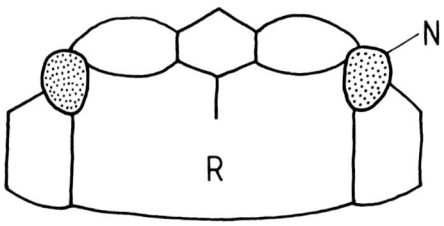

Figure 2 Tip of the snout of a gecko showing rostral scale (R) not touching nostrils (N)

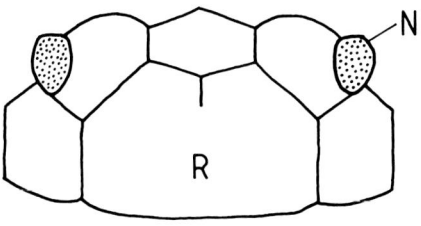

15a Less than 95 mm SVL; head not relatively large; irregular longitudinal striping present or absent; toes relatively narrow; males without pores on underside of thighs; not restricted to offshore islands ....
.... Pacific Gecko *Hoplodactylus pacificus* (p. 40)

15b May be 95 mm SVL or longer; if less than 95 mm SVL, the head seems disproportionately large; never striped; toes expanded to wide pads; males with pores on underside of thighs; restricted to offshore islands ....
.... Duvaucel's Gecko *Hoplodactylus duvaucelii* (p. 32)

Goldstripe Gecko
Hoplodactylus chrysosireticus   Robb, 1980

Description: Brown, olive-green or yellow-green with prominent, clearly defined longitudinal stripes. No irregular blotches. Two stripes come together abruptly at base of tail. Belly pale, often with fine black speckling. Rostral scale on tip of snout does not extend to nostrils (Fig. 2). Toes have expanded pads. Tail stout, often regrown. Males have one enlarged blunt scale on each side at base of tail.

Size: Up to about 70 mm SVL.

Distribution: North Island only. Coastal Taranaki from Waitara to Patea; Mana Island near Wellington.

Goldstripe Gecko   *Hoplodactylus chrysosireticus*

Habitat: Forest, scrub, coastal vegetation, farmland and gardens. Often in New Zealand flax or plants of similar form.

Habits: Nocturnal, but may sun-bask. Arboreal. Copulation takes place in April and young are born in February-March.

Notes: The specific name means 'gold-striped'. **Endangered.**

Duvaucel's Gecko
Hoplodactylus duvaucelii   (Duméril & Bibron, 1836)

Description: Mainly grey, often with a faint olive-green hue. Usually there are six pale, irregular blotches lying across the body from side to side between the back of the head and the base of the tail. Never striped. Toes have expanded pads. Tail stout, often regrown. Very heavy-bodied. Juveniles have larger heads than *H. pacificus* (p. 40) or *H. maculatus* (p. 37) of the same size.

Size: Up to 160 mm SVL. Weight up to about 120 g.

Distribution: Restricted to islands along the north-east coast of the North Island (including Great Barrier) and in the Cook Strait area (The Brothers, Chetwode and Trios groups). Subfossil bones attributed to this species have been found at widespread sites in the North and South Islands proving that the species was once more generally distributed.

Habitat: Forest, scrub, coastal vegetation and cliffs, often close to the shoreline. May forage on boulder beaches down to the splash zone.

Habits: Nocturnal but may sun-bask. Ground-dwelling or

Duvaucel's Gecko   *Hoplodactylus duvaucelii*

climbs to forage. Young are born between February and May and take about seven years to reach sexual maturity.

Notes: The largest living New Zealand lizard and one of the largest geckos in the world. An individual marked in the wild lived at least 36 years. The first specimens taken to Europe were thought to have come from Bengal, and the lizard was named after Alfred Duvaucel (1793?–1825), a French naturalist who explored parts of India.

Forest Gecko
Hoplodactylus granulatus
(Gray, 1845)

Description: Brightly coloured in grey, brown or reddish-brown, with much black and white, and sometimes yellowish patches. Back has a series of large irregular, transverse blotches usually without striping. Thin, dark, V-shaped mark on head between eyes. Bright white band runs from eye to ear on each side. Mouth lining orange or yellow. Much white along edges of mouth. Belly heavily blotched. Toes have slightly expanded pads. Soles of feet yellow.

Size: Up to 89 mm SVL.

Forest Gecko   *Hoplodactylus granulatus*

Distribution: Throughout mainland New Zealand (except the far north, Marlborough and Canterbury), and on some larger offshore islands (e.g., Great Barrier, Little Barrier, Waiheke and Kapiti).

Habitat: Forest and scrub, including beech forest and manuka scrub. Has been recorded up to 1400 m altitude.

Habits: Nocturnal but may sun-bask. Arboreal. Hides by day under loose bark or in crevices on the trunks or branches of trees. Forages at night in trees and bushes. Young are born in mid- to late summer.

Notes: About as widespread as the Common Gecko *H. maculatus*, but not as commonly found. The specific name refers to the animal's granular skin.

Black-eyed Gecko   *Hoplodactylus kahutarae*

Black-eyed Gecko
Hoplodactylus kahutarae   Whitaker, 1985

Description: Back dark olive-grey with six (rarely seven) pale, irregular blotches lying across body from side to side. Undersurfaces white. Eyes relatively large and totally black; surmounted by prominent ridges ('eyebrows'). Mouth lining pink; tongue reddish-yellow. Toes narrow, without distinctly enlarged pads; enlarged apical plates (beneath the toe next to the claw) absent from all toes.

Size: Up to 91 mm SVL.

Distribution: South Island only, in Seaward and Inland Kaikoura Ranges, Marlborough.

Habitat: Alpine bluffs and rocky outcrops. The few specimens known have been found at 1300–2200 m altitude.

Habits: Nocturnal but will sun-bask.

Notes: Named after the Kahutara Saddle where the type specimens were found. The only alpine lizard in New Zealand, occurring up to 400 m higher than any other species, in habitat commonly snow-bound for 3–5 months of the year. Can forage at lower air temperatures than other lizards – as low as 6°C. **Endangered.**

Common Gecko
Hoplodactylus maculatus   (Gray, 1845)

Description: Mainly grey or brown above with complex irregular markings that may include patches of black, white, yellow-orange and olive-green. Markings usually run from side to side across the body but some specimens have longitudinal striping as well. Belly pale and usually unspotted. Rostral scale on tip of snout does not extend to nostrils (Fig. 2). Snout-to-eye distance a little greater than, or equal to, eye-to-ear distance. Toes have expanded pads that extend further along the toes than in *H. pacificus* (p. 40). Tail stout, often regrown. Males have 1–2 enlarged blunt scales on each side at base of tail. Broad patch of preanal and femoral pores (along the undersurface of the thighs) in males.

Common Gecko   *Hoplodactylus maculatus*

Size: Up to 82 mm SVL.

Distribution: Widespread in the North Island, especially in coastal regions. Widespread throughout the South Island. Rare on Stewart Island.

Habitat: Forest, scrub and grassland. In coastal areas occurs closer to high-tide line than *H. pacificus*. Has been recorded up to 1700 m altitude.

Habits: Nocturnal but may sun-bask. Less arboreal than *H. pacificus*. Copulation occurs in April or May and the young are born between February and May.

Notes: Probably the most widespread and abundant New Zealand lizard. Recent studies of biochemical genetics have shown that the Common Gecko comprises several 'cryptic' species and these are likely to be described in the near future. The specific name means 'speckled', referring to distinctive spots on the type specimen. The average longevity of individuals studied in a wild population near Wellington was at least 13 years with some individuals reaching at least 17 years.

Cloudy Gecko
Hoplodactylus nebulosus   (McCann, 1955)

Description: Colour and pattern as for *H. granulatus* (p. 34) but usually more brown or green rather than grey, and pattern less distinct. Belly finely speckled. Snout more blunt and rounded than in *H. granulatus*.

Size: Not recorded, but similar to *H. granulatus*.

Distribution: Stewart Island and outliers.

Cloudy Gecko *Hoplodactylus nebulosus*

Habitat: Forest and scrub.

Habits: As for *H. granulatus*.

Notes: The specific name means 'cloudy', probably a reference to the colour and pattern.

Pacific Gecko
Hoplodactylus pacificus   (Gray, 1842)

Description: Colour and pattern as for *H. maculatus* (p. 37) but often brighter or less drab. Rostral scale on tip of snout extends to nostrils (Fig. 1). Snout-to-eye distance distinctly greater than eye-to-ear distance. Toes have expanded pads, but are more slender than in *H. maculatus* and have longer narrowed sections at the end. Tail stout, often regrown. Males have 3–4 enlarged pointed scales on each side at base of tail. Pores on the underside close to the vent of males are confined to small patches, not extending to the thighs as in other species. Resting animal has a more alert-looking posture than *H. maculatus*.

Size: Up to 94 mm SVL.

Distribution: North Island only: widespread throughout and on most northern offshore islands.

Habitat: Forest, scrub and grassland.

Habits: Strictly nocturnal. Hides in crevices by day and rarely sun-basks. At night may climb in vegetation to forage. Copulation takes place between March and May and young are born in February or March.

Pacific Gecko   *Hoplodactylus pacificus*

Notes: The specific name either refers to the Pacific area in which New Zealand lies, or means 'peaceful'.

Harlequin Gecko
Hoplodactylus rakiurae   Thomas, 1981

Description: Colour-pattern distinctively herring-boned with patches of dull green (or olive), brown and white. Broad, green, V-shaped mark between eyes. Mouth lining pinkish grey. Undersurfaces pale with black mottling and a purplish bloom. Toes plain brown and narrow, without distinctly enlarged pads. Enlarged apical plates (beneath the toe next to the claw) on all toes.

Size: Up to 71 mm SVL.

Distribution: Southern areas of Stewart Island.

Habitat: Wind-swept sub-alpine scrub with granite outcrops.

Habits: Nocturnal but will sun-bask. Arboreal.

Notes: The species was discovered in 1969. Named after Rakiura (Stewart Island). The Harlequin Gecko is one of the southernmost geckos in the world. **Endangered.**

Striped Gecko
Hoplodactylus stephensi   Robb, 1980

Description: Mainly brown with a similar distinctive striped pattern to *H. chrysosireticus* (p. 31). Rostral scale on tip of snout extends to nostrils (Fig. 1). Mouth lining pink, but skin at corners of (open) mouth orange. Toes have expanded pads. Males have 3 enlarged, pointed scales on each side at base of tail.

Size: Up to 80 mm SVL.

Harlequin Gecko   *Hoplodactylus rakiurae*

Striped Gecko *Hoplodactylus stephensi*

Distribution: Stephens and Maud Islands, Marlborough Sounds area.

Habitat: Coastal forest and scrub.

Habits: Nocturnal. Arboreal.

Notes: Named after Stephens Island. **Endangered.**

Common Green Gecko
Naultinus elegans   Gray, 1842

Description: Bright green above, often with large yellow, white or pale green patches on either side along the edge of the back. Sides often pale blue in adult males. Occasional specimens are bright yellow, a colour form probably analagous to

Common Green Gecko   *Naultinus elegans*

the albino in other animals. Belly pale green. Mouth lining dark blue; tongue blue. Toes narrow and tapering without expanded pads. Soles yellow. Tail slender; able to grip; seldom shed. Two subspecies: *punctatus* is larger and more heavily built than *elegans*. Undersurfaces of the feet and toes yellow in subspecies *punctatus*; grey-green in subspecies *elegans*.

Size: Up to 95 mm SVL.

Distribution: Subspecies *punctatus*: East Cape, Hawkes Bay and southern North Island. Subspecies *elegans*: rest of North Island (except Northland north of Whangaroa); Great and Little Barrier Islands.

Habitat: Forest and scrub. Commonly found in manuka and kanuka scrub.

Habits: Diurnal. Arboreal. The young of *punctatus* are born mainly in April and May; those of subspecies *elegans* in August.

Notes: The specific name means 'elegant'. The subspecific name *punctatus* means 'spotted'.

Jewelled Gecko
Naultinus gemmeus   (McCann, 1955)

Description: Bright green, usually with large white or yellow patches or stripes on either side along the edge of the back. Males from the Canterbury region are brown, grey and white with little green. Mouth lining blue. Toes narrow and tapering without expanded pads. Tail slender; able to grip; seldom shed.

Size: Up to 80 mm SVL.

Distribution: South Island (Canterbury, Otago and Southland) east of the Alps. Stewart Island.

Habitat: Forest, scrub and tussock grassland.

Jewelled Gecko   *Naultinus gemmeus*

Northland Green Gecko   *Naultinus grayii*

Habits: Diurnal. Arboreal. Copulation takes place in September-October and young are born between February and May.

Notes: The specific name is from the Latin for 'jewel'.

Northland Green Gecko
Naultinus grayii   Bell, 1843

Description: Vivid green above often with grey or gold-coloured markings on either side along the edge of the back. Males have a blue band along the sides just below the limbs. Undersurfaces pale green, sometimes with a yellow tinge. Mouth lining deep blue; tongue bright red. The scales on the snout are flat, rather than dome-shaped as in the Common Green Gecko (p. 43). Toes narrow and tapering without expanded pads. Tail slender; able to grip; seldom shed.

Size: Up to 95 mm SVL.

Distribution: Northland north of Whangaroa.

Habitat: Forest and scrub.

Habits: Diurnal. Arboreal. Copulation occurs in August-September and the young are born between March and June.

Notes: Named after John Edward Gray (1800–75) of the British Museum, who described several New Zealand lizards.

Marlborough Green Gecko
Naultinus manukanus   (McCann, 1955)

Description: Green above; more uniform and less highly patterned than most other South Island *Naultinus*. Mouth lining blue-tinged; tongue pink. Enlarged scales may be present on the head, nape, pelvic area and/or in rows along the sides but never over the entire body as in the Rough Gecko (overleaf). Toes narrow and tapering without expanded pads. Tail slender; able to grip; seldom shed.

Size: Up to 68 mm SVL.

Distribution: Marlborough region including Sounds, Stephens and D'Urville Islands.

Habitat: Forest and scrub. Often found on shrubs such as manuka, taupata and small-leaved divaricating species.

Habits: Diurnal. Arboreal. These lizards may copulate between June and October and give birth in March or April.

Marlborough Green Gecko   *Naultinus manukanus*

Notes: The specific name refers to manuka, a shrub on which this lizard is often found.

Rough Gecko
Naultinus rudis   (Fischer, 1882)

Description: Usually dark green above with white markings. (Males sometimes grey, brown or white with little or no green, similar to *N. gemmeus* from Canterbury, p. 45). Mouth lining dark blue; tongue greeny-yellow. Enlarged scales on the head and along the back, sides, tail and legs – some scales greatly enlarged. Toes narrow and tapering without expanded pads. Tail slender; able to grip; seldom shed.

Size: Up to 72 mm SVL.

Distribution: Inland Marlborough and north Canterbury.

Habitat: Forest and scrub.

Habits: Diurnal. Arboreal. Young are born in March or April.

Notes: The specific name means 'coarse' or 'rough' referring to irregular scales.

Rough Gecko *Naultinus rudis*

Nelson Green Gecko
Naultinus stellatus Hutton, 1872

Description: Colour and pattern especially variable. Usually green above with two broad stripes, or rows of diamond-shaped markings, running lengthwise along edges of back. These green or yellowish markings are usually outlined in darker colour. Some individuals are brown with dark green markings. Young are born green with white markings; within 18 months they change to the adult coloration. Toes narrow and tapering without expanded pads. Tail slender; able to grip; seldom shed.

Size: Up to 79 mm SVL.

Distribution: Wider Nelson area from Richmond Range to north-west Nelson, including Nelson Lakes district.

Habitat: Forest and scrub.

Habits: Diurnal. Arboreal. Young are born in autumn or early winter.

Notes: The specific name means 'starred', referring to the pattern.

Nelson Green Gecko *Naultinus stellatus*

West Coast Green Gecko
Naultinus tuberculatus   (McCann, 1955)

Description: Predominantly green above with a complex pattern of lighter and darker shades giving a 'mossy' appearance.

West Coast Green Gecko   *Naultinus tuberculatus*

Mouth lining blue; tongue orange-pink. Toes narrow, tapering without expanded pads. Tail slender; able to grip; seldom shed.

Size: Up to 85 mm SVL.

Distribution: Lewis Pass region, Rahu, Reefton and northern Westland.

Habitat: Forest and scrub.

Habits: Diurnal. Arboreal. Young are born between March and May.

Notes: The specific name means 'covered in tubercles', referring to enlarged scales on the head and body. Populations in the Lewis Pass area, Rahu and Reefton were named *Naultinus poecilochlorus* (Robb, 1980), but there seem to be insufficient grounds for treating them as a separate species.

Skinks

The skinks are a large family of lizards widely distributed in tropical and temperate parts of the world. The body scales are flat, shiny and overlapping (as in fish), the eyes small, and all New Zealand species have moveable lower eyelids. External differences between the sexes are subtle except when females are gravid.

All skinks in New Zealand give birth to live young, except the native Egg-laying Skink *Oligosoma suteri* and the introduced Rainbow Skink *Lampropholis delicata*, which lay eggs.

Skinks have long tails that they readily shed to escape predators. As in geckos, the regrown tail is never as long as the original and is slightly different in colour and pattern.

The native New Zealand skinks fall into two groups (see couplet 10 in the key). The *Oligosoma* skinks (formerly in the genus *Leiolopisma*) tend to have shallow pointed heads, bodies that are oval in cross-section and comparatively long limbs and toes. They usually prefer open habitats, are active by day (except *O. suteri*) and avidly sun-bask.

The *Cyclodina* skinks tend to have deeper, blunter heads, bodies that are squarish in cross-section and comparatively short limbs and toes. Usually they prefer shaded habitats, are nocturnal or crepuscular (active at dawn and dusk) and they are much less avid sun-baskers.

New Zealand skinks vary widely in size. Some never exceed 80 mm SVL (*Cyclodina aenea, C. ornata, Lampropholis delicata, Oligosoma inconspicuum, O. maccanni, O. microlepis, O. moco, O. nigriplantare* (except on the Chatham Islands where it grows to 91 mm SVL), *O. notosaurus, O. smithi, O. stenotis, O. striatum, O. zelandicum* and *Oligosoma* sp.). Others well exceed 80 mm SVL, the largest being *Cyclodina alani, Oligosoma fallai* and *O. homalonotum* which reach 140 mm SVL.

The New Zealand skinks are primarily carnivores, feeding on any arthropods (such as insects and spiders) that they can overpower. Most species also readily eat soft fruits when available or, in certain situations, carrion such as food regurgitated by seabirds.

KEY TO SKINKS

(For Cyclodina *skinks go straight to couplet 19)*

1a	Found in South or Stewart Islands	2
1b	Found in North Island	7
2a	Back very dark with many small greenish or yellowish flecks giving an overall greenish tinge; occurs on or very near exposed rocky shoreline platforms .... Fiordland Skink *Oligosoma acrinasum* (p. 67)	
2b	Not as above	3
3a	At least 40 longitudinal rows of scales around mid-body (use magnification)	4
3b	Less than 40 rows of mid-body scales	10
4a	Small (not larger than 67 mm SVL); toes very long relative to body size .... Long-toed Skink *Oligosoma* sp. (p. 90)	
4b	Large (adults exceeding 67 mm SVL); toes not long relative to body size .... (large South Island skinks)	5
5a	Upper surfaces dark with large pale patches and no fine speckling or, if finely speckled, there are large patches also; belly mottled .... Otago Skink *Oligosoma otagense* (p. 82)	
5b	Upper surfaces finely speckled with no large pale patches; belly plain, unmottled	6
6a	Base colour pale with dark speckling, often forming transverse bands; at least 54 longitudinal rows of scales around mid-body (use magnification) .... Scree Skink *Oligosoma waimatense* (p. 88)	

6b	Base colour dark with light speckling, often forming longitudinal lines; less than 54 rows of mid-body scales .... Grand Skink *Oligosoma grande* (p. 70)
7a	Edge of back flanked on either side by broad putty-coloured stripes that come close together at base of tail; belly heavily spotted .... Striped Skink *Oligosoma striatum* (p. 86)
7b	Not as above **8**
8a	Distinct chevron markings on back; bold black and white marks across 'lips'; rare, known only from Great and Little Barrier Islands .... Chevron Skink *Oligosoma homalonotum* (p. 71)
8b	Not as above **9**
9a	Back heavily blotched, no stripes; restricted to boulder or shingle beaches and rocky platforms; nocturnal .... Egg-laying Skink *Oligosoma suteri* (p. 87)
9b	Not as above **10**
10a	Body oval in cross-section; limbs and toes relatively long; head relatively shallow and pointed (Fig. 3); ear-opening usually with at least 1 projecting scale on forward margin (Fig. 3); lower eyelid with a large transparent disc (Fig. 3); discontinuous row of small scales below eye (Fig. 3); distinct stripe along mid-line of back (usually); no 'teardrop' marking below eye .... (*Lampropholis* and remaining *Oligosoma*) **11**
10b	Body squarish in cross-section; limbs and toes relatively short; head relatively deep and blunt (Fig. 4); ear-opening without projecting scales on forward margin (Fig. 4); lower eyelid usually lacking a single large, transparent disc (Fig. 4); row of small scales below eye usually continuous (Fig. 4); stripe along mid-line of back absent; white or yellowish spot edged in black ('teardrop') below eye (except *C. aenea*) .... (*Cyclodina*) **19**

Figure 3 Typical head of *Oligosoma* skinks showing relatively shallow head, disc on lower eyelid, discontinuous row of small scales below eye and projecting scales in ear opening

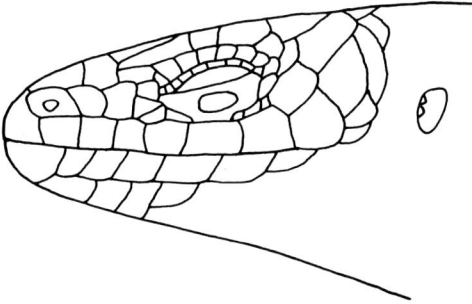

Figure 4 Typical head of *Cyclodina* skinks showing relatively deep head, no disc on lower eyelid, continuous row of small scales below eye and absence of projecting scales in ear opening

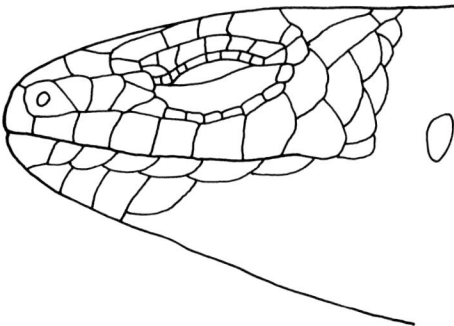

11a	Back scattered with distinctive white or pale green spots edged with black; eastern areas from Hawke's Bay to south Canterbury only .... Spotted Skink *Oligosoma lineoocellatum* (p. 75)
11b	Not as above **12**
12a	Back bright green flecked with black; Otago, Southland and Stewart Island only .... Green Skink *Oligosoma chloronoton* (p. 68)
12b	Not as above **13**
13a	Body with many longitudinal rows of scales – at least 38 rows at mid-body (use magnification); North Island only **14**
13b	Less than 38 mid-body scale rows **15**
14a	Small (up to 67 mm SVL); central North Island only .... Small-scaled Skink *Oligosoma microlepis* (p. 77)
14b	Large (up to 140 mm SVL); Three Kings Islands only .... Falla's Skink *Oligosoma fallai* (p. 69)
15a	Large, up to 106 mm SVL; belly heavily spotted .... Speckled Skink *Oligosoma infrapunctatum* (p. 74)
15b	Small, up to 80 mm SVL; belly plain or only faintly spotted **16**
16a	More speckled than striped; snout very pointed; never found far from shoreline; northern North Island only .... Shore Skink *Oligosoma smithi* (p. 83)
16b	Not as above **17**
17a	Ear-opening minute (not more than 0.9 mm across); few rows of scales at mid-body (26–29, use magnification); Stewart Island only .... Small-eared Skink *Oligosoma stenotis* (p. 84)
17b	Not as above **18**
18a	Back plain, not usually heavily speckled and no distinct stripe along mid-line; nasal scales (in which the nostrils lie) widely separated when viewed from above; up to 48 mm SVL; egg-laying; North Island only .... Rainbow Skink *Lampropholis delicata* (p. 66)

18b Back heavily speckled and/or with a distinct stripe along at least part of mid-line; nasal scales narrowly separated; up to 80 mm SVL; live-bearing .... remaining small brown *Oligosoma* skinks: *inconspicuum* and *maccanni* (South Island only); *notosaurus* (Stewart Island only); *moco* (North Island only); *nigriplantare* and *zelandicum*

19a Up to 80 mm SVL; 26–37 longitudinal rows of scales at mid-body (use magnification); North Island mainland and offshore islands **20**

19b Up to 142 mm SVL; 32–45 mid-body scale rows; North Island offshore islands only (except *C. whitakeri* at Pukerua Bay near Wellington) **21**

20a White or yellowish spot edged with black ('teardrop') below eye; may exceed 62 mm SVL .... Ornate Skink *Cyclodina ornata* (p. 63)

20b No 'teardrop' below eye; not longer than 62 mm SVL .... Copper Skink *Cyclodina aenea* (p. 58)

21a Belly heavily marked with flecks or blotches .... Marbled Skink *Cyclodina oliveri* (p. 61)

21b Belly lightly marked or unmarked **22**

22a Body very thickset and particularly squarish in cross-section; eye large relative to head-size; snout short; up to 142 mm SVL .... Robust Skink *Cyclodina alani* (p. 59)

22b Body less thickset and squarish; eye relatively small; snout elongate; up to 114 mm SVL **23**

23a Back with irregularly broken stripes; belly grey, cream or light pink .... McGregor's Skink *Cyclodina macgregori* (p. 60)

23b Back flecked but without stripes; belly yellow-orange .... Whitaker's Skink *Cyclodina whitakeri* (p. 64)

Copper Skink
Cyclodina aenea   Girard, 1857

Description: Back brown, often with a bright, copper-coloured stripe at the edges especially above the forelimbs. Jaw line flecked with black and white. Belly cream-coloured or yellowish-green; unspotted. Throat paler than belly; usually heavily spotted with black. Tail, especially underside, may be flushed with red. Otherwise very similar to *C. ornata* (p. 63) but 'teardrop' is absent, back and tail tend to lack large pale blotches (though may be speckled), and dorsolateral lines (at edges of back) are less broken.

Size: Up to 62 mm SVL.

Distribution: North Island only; widespread.

Habitat: Forest. Open or shaded areas with adequate ground-cover such as logs, rocks or long grass. In urban areas: compost heaps, rock gardens etc. Occurs close to the high-tide line in coastal situations.

Copper Skink   *Cyclodina aenea*

Habits: Active before dawn and throughout the day, but rarely emerges from cover. Young are born in late January and February. In one study the main foods were beetles, spiders and mites. Adults seem to remain in a small home range and exclude other adults.

Notes: New Zealand's smallest native lizard (but larger than the introduced Rainbow Skink). The commonest garden skink in Auckland and some suburbs of Wellington. The specific name means 'copper (or bronze) coloured'.

Robust Skink
Cyclodina alani   (Robb, 1970)

Description: Back brown with an irregular series of large, pale, dark-edged blotches which may extend onto sides. No prominent stripe along mid-line of back. Sides yellowish-grey with especially dark markings above the forelimbs. Yellow black-edged 'teardrop' below each eye. Snout blunt. Eye large and dark. Undersurface usually yellowish. However, in some individuals, the sides, throat and undersurfaces of the limbs are pink. Body very thickset. Tail very thick at base; tapering abruptly. Limbs and toes short and stubby.

Size: Up to 142 mm SVL. Weighs up to 60 g.

Distribution: North Island only. Restricted to north-eastern offshore islands: Motupia Island and Moturoa group off Northland; Green and Middle Islands in Mercury group off Coromandel Peninsula; and Castle Island off Coromandel Peninsula. Introduced by the Department of Conservation to Korapuki and Red Mercury Islands in the Mercury group, Coromandel Peninsula. Subfossil bones have been found in Northland, Waikato, Wairarapa, on Motutapu Island near

Robust Skink   *Cyclodina alani*

Auckland and on Mana Island near Wellington, proving that the species was once more widely distributed.

Habitat: Low coastal forest, where the lizards live in and around seabirds' burrows and under rocks and logs.

Habits: Nocturnal.

Notes: One of the three biggest New Zealand skinks. Named after the describer's nephew, Alan Robb. **Endangered.**

McGregor's Skink
Cyclodina macgregori   (Robb, 1975)

Description: Back dark brown; plain or with elongate, darker markings giving a streaked effect. Sides irregularly marked with dark and pale blotches merging into a very dark area above the forelimbs. Pale, black-edged 'teardrop' below each eye. Undersurfaces grey, cream-coloured or pale pink.

Size: Up to 112 mm SVL.

Distribution: North Island only. Restricted to offshore islands: the Cavalli group and Bream Islands off Northland; Sail Rock in the Hauraki Gulf; and Mana Island north of Wellington. Subfossil bones have been found in Northland and Waikato, proving that the species was once more generally distributed.

Habitat: Leaf-litter under coastal forest and scrub.

Habits: Nocturnal.

Notes: Named after Professor William Roy McGregor (1895–1975), former head of the Zoology Department, University of Auckland. **Endangered.**

McGregor's Skink   *Cyclodina macgregori*

Marbled Skink
Cyclodina oliveri   (McCann, 1955)

Description: Back light or dark brown, often speckled but without a prominent stripe along mid-line. Edges of back

Marbled Skink   *Cyclodina oliveri*

may be copper-coloured along the front half of the body.
Sides very dark above forelimbs; otherwise dark grey or
brown, heavily speckled with black and white. White black-
edged 'teardrop' below each eye. Belly pale yellowish or
faintly red-tinged; usually speckled. Throat white, often
densely speckled or streaked. Tail thick; relatively short;
tapering abruptly.

Size: Up to 114 mm SVL.

Distribution: North Island only. Restricted to north-eastern offshore islands: Poor Knights, Mokohinau, Hen and Chickens, Great and Little Barrier, Mercury, Ohena and Aldermen Islands.

Habitat: Leaf-litter under coastal forest and scrub.

Habits: Largely nocturnal. Occasionally forages in daylight but rarely sun-basks.

Notes: Also known as Oliver's Skink. Named after Dr W.R.B. Oliver (1883–1957), former Director of the Dominion Museum (now Museum of New Zealand), Wellington. Genetic studies indicate that some island populations (Mokohinau, Hen and Chickens) may be distinct species.

Ornate Skink
Cyclodina ornata   (Gray, 1843)

Description: Brown above with no distinct stripe along midline of back. Large, pale blotches along top and sides of tail, often extending onto back. Undersurfaces yellowish often with reddish tinges; unspotted, or partly or wholly spotted with black. White or yellowish 'teardrop' edged with black below each eye. Snout short and blunt. Tail thick; relatively short.

Size: Up to 80 mm SVL.

Distribution: North Island only; widespread but less common than *C. aenea*.

Habitat: Forest or open areas with stable cover such as deep rock piles.

Habits: Nocturnal/crepuscular (active at dawn and dusk). Young are born in late January and February. In one study the main foods were beetles, spiders, mites, small snails and plant matter. Adults seem to remain in a small home range and exclude other adults.

Notes: The specific name means 'ornate'.

Whitaker's Skink
Cyclodina whitakeri   Hardy, 1977

Description: Back yellow-brown without a prominent stripe along mid-line. Sides yellowish; heavily mottled with black especially above forelimbs and towards head. White black-edged 'teardrop' below each eye. Belly yellowish-orange; throat grey. Sides and top of tail may be orange-tinged.

Size: Up to 101 mm SVL. Weighs up to 20 g.

Distribution: North Island only. Originally known from three localities: Middle Island in Mercury group off Coromandel Peninsula; Castle Island off Coromandel Peninsula; and Pukerua Bay on mainland north of Wellington. Introduced to Korapuki (1988) and Red Mercury Islands (1994), in the Mercury group, by the Department of Conservation. Subfossil bones have been found in Waikato, proving that the species was once more generally distributed.

Habitat: Coastal forest and scrub, where the lizards live in and around seabird burrows and in layers of leaf-litter. At Pukerua Bay the population is restricted to a vegetated boulder bank.

Habits: Largely nocturnal and crepuscular (active at dawn

Ornate Skink   *Cyclodina ornata*

and dusk). Occasionally forages in daylight but rarely sun-basks.

Notes: Named after Tony Whitaker (1944–   ) who has studied New Zealand lizards for 30 years. **Endangered.**

Whitaker's Skink   *Cyclodina whitakeri*

Rainbow Skink
Lampropholis delicata   (De Vis, 1888)

Description: Back brown, usually plain without a stripe along mid-line and without much speckling. A dark brown band runs along each side of the body and may be bordered above (or above and below) by paler striping. Undersurfaces whitish; usually unspotted. Tail particularly long and thin. The nasal scales (in which the nostrils lie) are widely separated, more so than in *Oligosoma*.

Rainbow Skink   *Lampropholis delicata*

Size: Up to 55 mm SVL.

Distribution: Eastern Australia, including Tasmania. Introduced to Hawaii. In New Zealand (introduced) presently restricted to North Island: Auckland, Waikato, Coromandel Peninsula and Bay of Plenty.

Habitat: Open areas, such as suburban gardens, grassland and industrial sites, with adequate cover (logs, stones, grass etc.); also lightly wooded areas.

Habits: Diurnal. Terrestrial; usually found in leaf-litter and among debris on the ground. Egg-laying; the eggs are 8–10 mm long, oval with a tough, white, leathery shell, and are deposited beneath logs or stones. There are 2–5 eggs in a clutch but females may lay communally to produce aggregations of eggs. Young hatch in February and March.

Notes: The smallest lizard in New Zealand. The specific name means 'delicate'. Introduced. Probably arrived accidentally at Auckland in cargo in the 1960s and spread from there in freight. Likely to spread further.

Fiordland Skink
Oligosoma acrinasum   (Hardy, 1977)

Description: Dark brown to black above, with a multitude of small yellow or green flecks giving an overall greenish tinge. Belly mottled with greenish-grey and black.

Size: Up to 85 mm SVL.

Distribution: Known only from small islands off south-west Fiordland and one adjacent mainland site.

Fiordland Skink   *Oligosoma acrinasum*

Green Skink   *Oligosoma chloronoton*

Habitat: Exposed rocky shoreline platforms and boulder beaches.

Habits: Diurnal. Extremely avid sun-basker. Seeks cover in rocky cracks and crevices and may enter splash pools to escape danger. Eats marine invertebrates.

Notes: The specific name means 'pointed-nosed'. The only New Zealand lizard that sun-basks communally – more than 30 may bask together in a pile.

Green Skink
Oligosoma chloronoton   (Hardy, 1977)

Description: Back deep green with black and light green flecks. Dorsolateral stripes (at edges of back) copper or light brown. Sides black with lighter flecks. Undersurfaces grey; some specimens have a dark-spotted throat.

Size: Up to 108 mm SVL.

Distribution: South Island only: Otago, Southland and Stewart Island.

Habitat: Tussock grassland, scrub, boulder fields and coastal vegetation.

Habits: Diurnal. Avid sun-basker.

Notes: The specific name means 'green-backed'.

Falla's Skink
Oligosoma fallai   (McCann, 1955)

Description: Back golden brown; sides have a dark brown band. Upper surfaces heavily speckled with light and dark flecks. Chin and throat greyish; belly yellowish. Undersurfaces usually black-spotted. Robust. Tail very thick at base.

Falla's Skink   *Oligosoma fallai*

Size: Up to 140 mm SVL.

Distribution: Known only from the Three Kings Islands north-west of Cape Reinga.

Habitat: Coastal forest, scrub and low-growing vegetation.

Habits: Diurnal. In seabird colonies readily eats carrion.

Notes: One of the three biggest New Zealand skinks. Named after Sir Robert Falla (1901–79), a prominent New Zealand naturalist.

Grand Skink
Oligosoma grande   (Gray, 1845)

Description: Upper surfaces of body, tail and legs black with numerous cream-coloured or greenish flecks in longitudinal

Grand Skink   *Oligosoma grande*

rows. Pale dorsolateral lines (along edges of back) may be present. Belly cream-coloured; not mottled. Throat faintly marked in black.

Size: Up to 109 mm SVL. Weighs up to 29 g.

Distribution: Otago only; widespread but very rare.

Habitat: Rocky outcrops in tussock grassland.

Habits: Diurnal. Very active and agile, retreating into cracks and crevices if alarmed.

Notes: The specific name means 'significantly large'. **Endangered.**

Chevron Skink
Oligosoma homalonotum   (Boulenger, 1906)

Description: Back and sides reddish brown or greyish. Light and dark patches form a distinct row of chevron markings along the back and tail (apexes of chevrons point towards head). Never striped. Alternating black and white bands form a distinct pattern across 'lips'. Undersurfaces pale with scattered spots especially on throat. Intact tail long and slender.

Size: Up to 143 mm SVL.

Distribution: Great and Little Barrier Islands.

Habitat: Stream margins in native forest.

Habits: Diurnal.

Notes: One of the three biggest New Zealand skinks. The specific name means 'smooth-backed'. **Endangered.**

Cryptic Skink
Oligosoma inconspicuum
(Patterson & Daugherty, 1990)

Description: Reddish brown above with longitudinal stripes and much speckling. Underparts yellowish. Chin usually speckled.

Size: Up to 70 mm SVL.

Distribution: Otago and Southland. Sea-level to an altitude of 1700 m.

Cryptic Skink   *Oligosoma inconspicuum*

Chevron Skink *Oligosoma homalonotum*

Habitat: Prefers areas of herbs and shrubs rather than grass-land. Tolerates relatively damp substrates.

Habits: Diurnal. Young are born in late January and February.

Notes: The specific name means 'not readily visible', referring to the difficulty of distinguishing this species from its close relatives.

Speckled Skink   *Oligosoma infrapunctatum*

Speckled Skink
Oligosoma infrapunctatum   (Boulenger, 1887)

Description: Brown. Striped but heavily speckled as well, such that the longitudinal stripes and bands have irregular, speckled margins. Undersurfaces pale grey, yellowish or orange; heavily spotted. Robust.

Size: Up to 106 mm SVL.

Distribution: Widespread but very localised: Whale Island and inland Bay of Plenty, Waikato, central North Island, Wairarapa, Stephens Island, Nelson area and northern Westland.

Habitat: Open forest, scrubby areas and tussock country.

Habits: Diurnal.

Notes: The specific name means 'spotted below'.

Spotted Skink
Oligosoma lineoocellatum (Duméril & Duméril, 1851)

Description: Back brown, olive green or bright green, with distinctive pale green spots edged in black. Dorsolateral stripes (at edges of back) usually prominent. Belly grey, pink or red; unspotted. Throat grey with black spots.

Size: Up to 111 mm SVL.

Distribution: North Island: restricted to eastern areas from Hawke's Bay to Wellington. South Island: widespread in eastern areas from Nelson and the Marlborough Sounds to south Canterbury.

Habitat: Open grassy or scrubland areas from sea level to the sub-alpine zone.

Habits: Diurnal. Avid sun-basker.

Notes: The specific name refers to the rows of eye-like spots on the back.

Spotted Skink   *Oligosoma lineoocellatum*

McCann's Skink
Oligosoma maccanni (Hardy, 1977)

Description: Back light brown or grey with lighter and darker stripes.

Size: Up to 73 mm SVL.

Distribution: South Island only: east of the divide from mid-Canterbury to Southland. From sea-level to an altitude of 1500 m.

Habitat: Dry, rocky areas in tussock grassland and scrub. The lizards shelter under rocks or in vegetation such as wild spaniards (*Aciphylla*).

Habits: Diurnal. Avid sun-basker. Young are born in late January and February.

Notes: Named after Charles McCann (1899–1980), vertebrate zoologist at the Dominion Museum (now Museum of New Zealand), Wellington, who

McCann's Skink   *Oligosoma maccanni*

Small-scaled Skink   *Oligosoma microlepis*

published the first major revision of New Zealand lizards in 1955.

Small-scaled Skink
Oligosoma microlepis   (Patterson & Daugherty, 1990)

Description: Grey-brown above with prominent longitudinal stripes and speckling. Undersurfaces pale, unspeckled. Longitudinal rows of scales at mid-body numerous (use magnification) – 38–44. Soles grey.

Size: Up to 67 mm SVL.

Distribution: Known only from the central North Island – Moawhango, Rangitikei and Taruarau River catchments and Motutaiko Island in Lake Taupo.

Habitat: Boulder river beds and grassy areas with loose rocks for cover.

Habits: Diurnal. Avid sun-basker. Young are born between late January and early March.

Notes: The specific name means 'small-scaled' – this species has small body scales and a large number of rows of scales at the mid-body compared to its relatives of similar size. **Endangered.**

Moko Skink
Oligosoma moco   (Duméril & Bibron, 1839)

Description: Brown with prominent pale and dark longitudinal stripes and bands with regular margins. Occasional specimens are very dark, almost black. There may be an X-shaped mark on the head. Undersurfaces pale; unspotted or virtually so. Intact tail particularly long.

Size: Up to 73 mm SVL.

Distribution: North Island only: widespread on north-eastern offshore islands; occurs at a few mainland localities in Northland, Auckland and Bay of Plenty. Not found south of the Bay of Plenty.

Habitat: Open forest and scrub.

Moko Skink   *Oligosoma moco*

Habits: Diurnal. Avid sun-basker.

Notes: The specific name derives from moko, the Maori word for lizard.

Common Skink
Oligosoma nigriplantare   (Peters, 1873)

Description: Brown with prominent stripes. Often highly speckled. Occasionally very dark brown or almost black. Underside grey or yellowish; usually unspotted; never suffused with red or orange as in *O. zelandicum* (p. 90). Regrown tail may be reddish above and below. Snout fairly blunt. Pattern varies greatly from region to region. For example, the stripes are clear with regular margins in specimens from Otago and Southland, but broken with irregular margins in individuals from the North Island and northern South Island. Specimens from the Chatham Islands vary in colour (green, brown or black) and many lack longitudinal stripes.

Size: Up to 77 mm SVL on the mainland (subspecies *polychroma*) or 91 mm SVL on the Chatham Islands (subspecies *nigriplantare*).

Distribution: Hawkes Bay and central to southern parts of the North Island; throughout the South Island; Stewart Island (subspecies *polychroma*). Chatham Islands (subspecies *nigriplantare*).

Habitat: Dry, open areas with low vegetation or debris such as logs or stones for cover. Common in coastal areas, shingle riverbeds, tussock grassland, farmland, urban areas. Found to an altitude of 1700 m.

Habits: Diurnal. Avid sun-basker. Young are born in January and February.

Notes: The common garden skink in many parts of the southern North Island and South Island. The only lizard known from the Chatham Islands. The specific name means 'black-soled', which can be misleading since many have yellowish soles.

Common Skink   *Oligosoma nigriplantare*

Southern Skink   *Oligosoma notosaurus*

Southern Skink
Oligosoma notosaurus   (Patterson & Daugherty, 1990)

Description: Dark brown above with darker and lighter longitudinal stripes and flecking. Undersurfaces grey-brown with pronounced black speckling on the throat.

Size: Up to 76 mm SVL.

Distribution: Known only from the Stewart Island area, including Codfish Island.

Otago Skink   *Oligosoma otagense*

Habitat: Scrub and open habitat, rocky areas. Specimens have been collected between sea-level and an altitude of 700 m.

Habits: Diurnal.

Notes: The specific name means 'southern lizard'.

Otago Skink
Oligosoma otagense   (McCann, 1955)

Description: Black above with large distinctive cream-coloured or greenish blotches on the back, sides, limbs and tail. Undersurfaces light grey or yellowish with distinctive black mottling. Soles dark brown. Very robust in all proportions.

Size: Up to 124 mm SVL.

Distribution: Otago only; widespread but very localised and rare.

Habitat: Rocky outcrops in tussock grassland.

Habits: Diurnal. Sun-basks on sunny ledges and retreats into cracks if disturbed.

Notes: The largest South Island skink. Named after Otago Province. **Endangered.**

Shore Skink
Oligosoma smithi   (Gray, 1845)

Description: Upper surfaces grey, brown or greenish; heavily speckled. Striping, if present, is usually weak. Some specimens entirely black. Belly grey, cream-coloured, reddish or black; occasionally lightly spotted. Snout very pointed.

Size: Up to 80 mm SVL.

Distribution: North Island only: west coast north of Muriwai Beach (near Auckland); east coast north of Gisborne; widespread on northern offshore islands.

Habitat: Never far from shoreline. Prefers open areas, for example, driftwood at high-tide mark, mat-forming vegetation in sand-dunes, pasture beside the shore.

Habits: Strongly diurnal, retreating into low vegetation or beneath logs, stones or other debris if disturbed. Forages to intertidal zone at low water.

Notes: The common beach skink of northern New Zealand. Also known as Smith's Skink. Named after Lieutenant Alexander Smith of the Royal Navy who was associated with the expedition that collected the original specimens in the 1840s.

Small-eared Skink
Oligosoma stenotis
(Patterson & Daugherty, 1994)

Description: Brown above, often with a striking pale green coloration. Strongly striped longitudinally; stripes fairly wide. Longitudinal rows of scales at mid-body few (use magnification) – 26–29. Ear

Shore Skink   *Oligosoma smithi*

Small-eared Skink   *Oligosoma stenotis*

opening minute (not wider than 0.9 mm). Undersurfaces greyish or greenish.

Size: Up to 75 mm SVL.

Distribution: Known only from Stewart Island.

Habitat: Sub-alpine scrub to 700 m above sea-level.

Habits: Nothing known.

Notes: The specific name means 'narrow-eared'.

Striped Skink
Oligosoma striatum   (Buller, 1871)

Description: Back pale brown with a double row of white spots edged in black; flanked on either side by a broad, putty-coloured stripe arising above the eye and running along the body and tail. These two bands converge abruptly at the base of the tail. Undersurfaces pale or yellowish; heavily speckled with dark brown or black.

Size: Up to 76 mm SVL.

Distribution: North Island only: southern Northland, Waitakere Ranges, Little and Great Barrier Islands, Rotorua district, King Country and inland Taranaki.

Habitat: Fallen rotting logs lying in native forest or remaining in pasture after the bush is cleared. Also found in forest canopy in epiphytes and standing dead trees.
Habits: Diurnal. At least partly arboreal.

Notes: Has probably declined with the clearance of native

Striped Skink   *Oligosoma striatum*

Egg-laying Skink   *Oligosoma suteri*

forests. Populations living in pasture may die out when the fallen logs rot away. The specific name means 'streaked'. **Endangered.**

Egg-laying Skink
Oligosoma suteri   (Boulenger, 1906)

Description: Back, sides and limbs grey or brown, heavily blotched with black or dark brown. Some specimens entirely black. Never striped. Undersurfaces greyish, occasionally pink or bright orange; sometimes black-spotted. 'Cheek' region between eye and ear may seem swollen when animal viewed from above.

Size: Up to 108 mm SVL.

Distribution: North Island only: widespread on north-eastern offshore islands from Three Kings to Aldermen Islands; occurs at a few mainland sites from Cape Reinga to Port Jackson.

Habitat: Entirely restricted to boulder or shingle beaches and rocky platforms in the splash zone.

Habits: Nocturnal but may sun-bask. Hides by day in crevices or under piles of seaweed. May enter splash pools while foraging, or to escape danger. A good swimmer. Egg-laying; 3–4 eggs are laid beneath large stones in hollows in the silt, sand or gravel substrate. Eggs are oval with a tough white, leathery shell. They are about 15 mm long and 10 mm wide at laying, but swell by up to a third before hatching. Laying is in summer and hatching in autumn; incubation period is three months. Several females may share a nest.

Notes: The only native lizard that lays eggs. Named after Henry Suter (1841–1918), a New Zealand conchologist (expert on mollusc shells).

Scree Skink
Oligosoma waimatense   (McCann, 1955)

Description: Pale yellow-brown or grey above with longitudinal streaking as in *O. grande* (p. 71). However, dark areas coalesce to produce thin, irregular black bands running across back and down sides. Pale dorsolateral lines (along edges of back) may be present. Belly grey or tinged with orange or pink; unspotted. Chin and throat may be lightly black-spotted. Soles pale brown to black. Moderately robust but lighter in build and thinner at base of tail than *O. otagense* (p. 82).

Scree Skink *Oligosoma waimatense*

Size: Up to 107 mm SVL.

Distribution: South Island only: inland areas of Marlborough, Canterbury and Otago.

Habitat: Open rocky areas, dry stream beds and screes in semi-arid tussock country. To an altitude of 1400 m.

Habits: Diurnal. Avid sun-basker.

Notes: Named after Waimate where the type specimen was collected. **Endangered.**

Brown Skink
Oligosoma zelandicum   (Gray, 1843)

Description: Back pale brown; sides darker brown. Some shoreline populations are black. Belly grey, straw-coloured or suffused with red or orange; sometimes spotted. Throat usually black-spotted. Soles dark brown or black. Sides and underparts of tail and hindlimbs sometimes reddish.

Size: Up to 73 mm SVL.

Distribution: North Island: west of the ranges from Taranaki to Wellington. South Island: Marlborough Sounds, Nelson, north Westland.

Habitat: Forest, or shady, moist situations in farmland or gardens.

Habits: Diurnal.

Notes: The specific name refers to New Zealand.

Long-toed Skink
Oligosoma sp.

Description: Back grey brown with brown and grey blotches; sides darker brown. Stripes usually present along sides but rarely along mid-line of back. Belly grey with dark speckles, especially under chin. Longitudinal rows of scales at mid-body numerous (use magnification) – 40–44.

Size: Up to 67 mm SVL.

Distribution: South Island only: known only from a few

Brown Skink   *Oligosoma zelandicum*

localities in Marlborough and Canterbury.

Habitat: Dry rocky places, boulder tumbles, eroding river terraces.

Habits: Diurnal.

Notes: Though recognised for many years, this species has not yet been described and named.

Long-toed Skink   *Oligosoma* sp.

Marine Reptiles

Sea-turtles and sea-snakes are widespread in tropical and sub-tropical seas of the world, and from time to time they occur in cold waters. Some of the turtles may deliberately seek out temperate waters as feeding grounds. Marine reptiles are most often found in northern New Zealand. They may be seen at sea, accidentally caught in nets or found cast ashore in a sick, injured or exhausted state. Those reported are probably only a fraction of the actual numbers; many others are likely to go unnoticed.

Sea-snakes are distinguished from land snakes by their adaptations for aquatic life – a paddle-shaped tail, and nostrils that seal to prevent water entering between breaths. The species that reach New Zealand have toxic venom, and if found alive they should be treated with caution. No marine reptiles are known to breed in New Zealand, or are likely to do so.

KEY TO MARINE REPTILES
(sea-snakes and turtles)

1a   Limbs and carapace (shell) present .... (Turtles) **2**

1b   Limbs and carapace absent .... (Sea-snakes) **6**

2a   Limbs without claws; paddles relatively large; carapace with several prominent longitudinal ridges ....
.... Leathery Turtle *Dermochelys coriacea* (p. 94)

2b   Limbs with claws; paddles moderate size; carapace with 1 longitudinal ridge along mid-line of back, or no ridges **3**

3a   4 costal shields on each side of carapace **4**

3b   5 or more costal shields on each side **5**

4a   2 pairs of prefrontal shields on head; shields of carapace usually overlapping like tiles; tip of upper jaw projecting forwards and downwards to form a narrow 'beak' ....
.... Hawksbill Turtle *Eretmochelys imbricata* (p. 100)

4b   1 pair of prefrontals; shields of carapace not overlapping; tip of upper jaw not beaked ....
.... Green Turtle *Chelonia mydas* (p. 98)

5a   5 (rarely 6) costal shields on each side of carapace; adults reddish-brown above; usually 3 enlarged shields (inframarginals) on each side at the outer edge of the underside of the 'shell' between the fore and hind limbs ....
.... Loggerhead Turtle *Caretta caretta* (p. 96)

5b   6 or more costal shields on each side; adults olive-grey above; 4 enlarged inframarginals ....
.... Olive Ridley Turtle *Lepidochelys olivacea* (p. 102)

6a   Alternating dark and light bands around the body; snout small and blunt; belly scales much larger than back scales ....
.... Banded Sea-snake *Laticauda colubrina* (p. 103)

6b   Back dark, belly pale, without transverse bands; snout long; belly scales similar size to back scales ....
.... Yellow-bellied Sea-snake *Pelamis platurus* (p. 104)

Leathery Turtle
Dermochelys coriacea   (Vandelli, 1761)

Description: Predominantly dark (brown or black) above; pale below. May be blotched especially on the sides, neck and underparts. Carapace (shell) a mosaic of small, many-sided bony plates covered in leathery skin. Carapace has seven longitudinal ridges (including those at the sides). Limbs clawless; front paddles relatively enormous (Fig. 5). Upper jaw deeply notched.

Size: Carapace up to 1.8 m long. Up to 2.8 m total length. Weighs up to 700 kg, more usually about 500 kg.

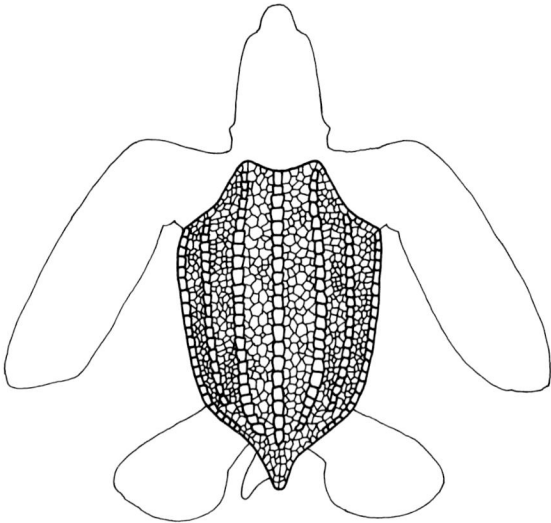

Figure 5   Silhouette of Leathery Turtle showing carapace, relatively enormous paddles and clawless limbs

Leathery Turtle   *Dermochelys coriacea*

Distribution: All tropical and temperate seas. Relatively regular visitor to New Zealand, reported as far south as Foveaux Strait. First recorded 1892; more than 25 records since 1930. Recent records include Little Barrier Island (1986); Mahuta Gap near Dargaville (1989); Cape Runaway (1990); Cape Brett (1992); Waitemata Harbour (1993).

Habits: Normally comes ashore only to lay eggs.

Notes: The largest of all living turtles. The commonest turtle in New Zealand waters. Foods include salps and jellyfish. The specific name means 'leathery'.

Loggerhead Turtle
Caretta caretta   (Linnaeus, 1758)

Description: Brown or red-brown above; pale below. Shields of carapace (shell) lie side by side (not overlapping) in adults. Carapace has five (rarely six or more) pairs of costal shields (Fig. 6). Head has two pairs of prefrontal shields (as for the Hawksbill Turtle, Fig. 8).

Size: Carapace up to about 1.1 m long. Weighs up to 182 kg.

Distribution: Throughout the tropics, and venturing into temperate waters. Occasional visitor to New Zealand. First recorded 1885; about 12 records since 1950. Recent records include Masons Bay, Stewart Island (1986); Piha Beach near

Loggerhead Turtle   *Caretta caretta*

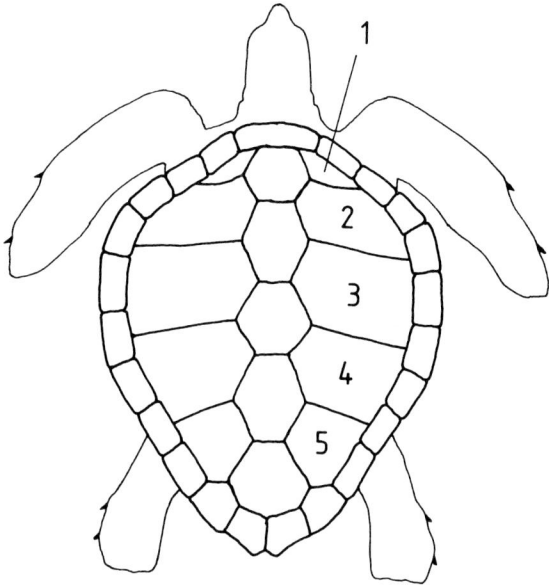

Figure 6 Silhouette of Loggerhead Turtle showing 5 costal shields

Auckland (1986); Himatangi Beach near Foxton (1989); Otaki Beach (1990); Devonport (1990).

Notes: The latinised name 'caretta' is from the Spanish meaning 'tortoise-shell'. Eats crabs and molluscs.

Green Turtle
Chelonia mydas   (Linnaeus, 1758)

Description: Adult olive or brown above; yellowish or white below. Shields of carapace (shell) lie side by side (not overlapping). Carapace has four pairs of costal shields (Fig. 7). Head has one pair of prefrontal shields (Fig. 7).

Size: Carapace up to about 1.1 m long. Weighs up to 182 kg.

Distribution: Throughout the tropics. A common, non-breeding resident around the Kermadec Islands. Occasional visitor to northern New Zealand; once recorded at Banks

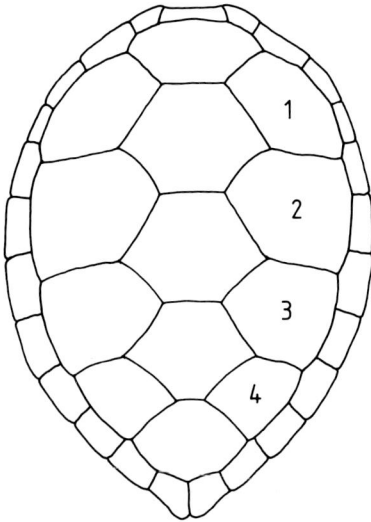

Figure 7   Carapace of Green Turtle (below) showing 4 costal shields. Head of Green Turtle (right) showing single pair of prefrontal shields

Green Turtle   *Chelonia mydas*

Peninsula (1987). First recorded 1895; more than 12 records since 1980. Recent records include Te Kopuru, near Dargaville (1988); Waitemata Harbour (1989); Waiheke Island (1989); Hauraki Gulf (1988 and 1990).

Notes: Its common name derives from its fat, which imparts a green colouring to turtle soup. A herbivore, feeding mainly on seaweed and seagrass.

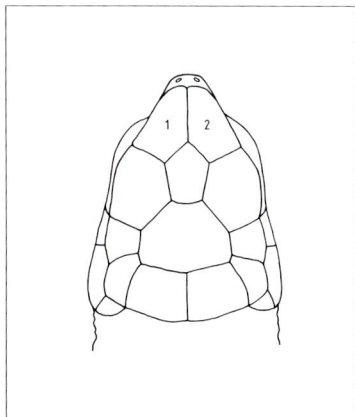

Hawksbill Turtle
Eretmochelys imbricata   (Linnaeus, 1766)

Description: Carapace (shell) of adult strongly variegated or marbled with shades of brown. Yellow below. Edge of carapace strongly serrated except in old individuals. Shields of carapace strongly overlapping except in old individuals (where side by side). Carapace has four pairs of costal shields (Fig. 8). Head has two pairs of prefrontal shields (Fig. 8). Upper jaw beaked.

Size: Carapace up to about 0.9 m long. Weighs up to 64 kg.

Distribution: Throughout the tropics near coral or rocky reefs or in shallow bays and lagoons. Occasional visitor to

Figure 8   Carapace of Hawksbill Turtle (below) showing 4 costal shields. Head of Hawksbill Turtle (right) showing 2 pairs of prefrontal shields

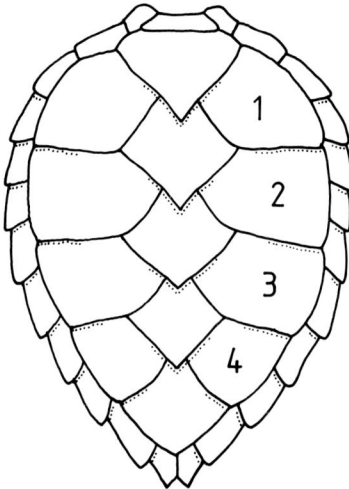

Hawksbill Turtle *Eretmochelys imbricata*

northern New Zealand; once recorded at Palliser Bay (1982). First recorded 1949; at least six records since 1980. Recent records include Rakino Island in the Hauraki Gulf (1987); Muriwai Beach (1988); Ahipara (1989); Cape Colville (1989).

Notes: The 'tortoise-shell' of commerce comes from this species. The specific name means 'overlapping like tiles', a reference to the shields of the carapace. Eats molluscs and crustaceans.

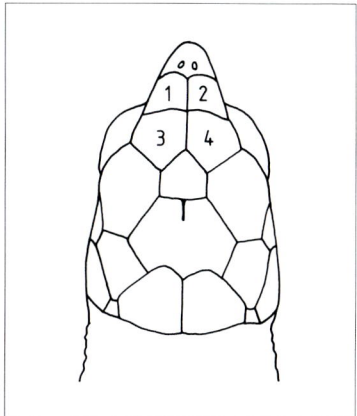

Olive Ridley Turtle

Lepidochelys olivacea (Eschscholtz, 1829)

Description: Upper surfaces grey or grey-green. Underparts whitish. Head relatively large. Carapace (shell) has usually six or more pairs of costal shields. Head has two pairs of pre-frontal shields (as for Hawksbill Turtle, Fig. 8).

Size: Carapace up to about 0.7 m long. Weighs up to 41 kg.

Distribution: Tropical regions of the Indian, Pacific and south Atlantic Oceans. Rare visitor to New Zealand; known from only two records: Wellington district (1956) and Kaka Point Beach, near Balclutha (1985).

Notes: The rarest and smallest turtle in New Zealand waters. Eats crustaceans, fish eggs and plant material.

Olive Ridley Turtle *Lepidochelys olivacea*

Banded Sea-snake   *Laticauda colubrina*

Banded Sea-snake
Laticauda colubrina   (Schneider, 1799)

Description: Bluish-grey above, yellowish below, with about 35 prominent, black cross-bands. Head small and blunt (Fig. 9). Row of broad scales along belly, more than half the width of the body. Tail compressed sideways to form a paddle.

Figure 9   Side of head of Banded Sea-snake showing blunt snout

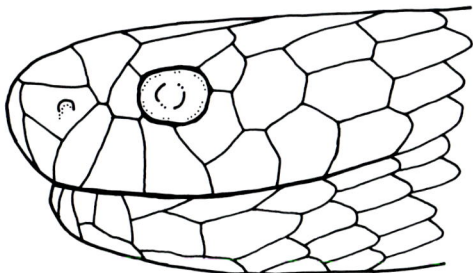

Size: Up to about 1.4 m total length.

Distribution: India, south-east Asia, New Guinea, Australia and Pacific Islands. Rare visitor to New Zealand; fewer than 10 records since the first in 1880. Recent records include Castlepoint (1977); Whangaruru Harbour, Northland (1990); Ohope Beach, Bay of Plenty (1990).

Habits: In its usual range this species is partly terrestrial, often occurring among rocks near the shore, or in mangrove swamps some distance inland. Largely nocturnal. Unlike all other sea-snakes, which produce live young, members of this genus lay eggs on land.

Notes: Also known as Banded Sea Krait. The specific name means 'serpent-like'. **Venomous.**

Yellow-bellied Sea-snake
Pelamis platurus   (Linnaeus, 1766)

Description: Upper half of body dark; lower half yellowish. The two colours usually meet abruptly to form a straight line along each side. Head elongate (Fig. 10). Belly scales similar size to other body-scales. Tail compressed sideways to form a paddle; yellowish with large dark spots.

Size: Up to about 1 m total length.

Distribution: Indian and Pacific Oceans. Relatively regular visitor to northern New Zealand, and occasionally found as far south as Taranaki, Wairarapa coast and Nelson. First recorded 1837; more than 35 records since 1930. Recent records include Stony Bay, Coromandel Peninsula (1987); Muriwai Beach (1988); Manukau Heads (1989); Baylys Beach

Yellow-bellied Sea-snake   *Pelamis platurus*

near Dargaville (1989); Whakatane River mouth (1989);
Ninety Mile Beach (1991).

Habits: Truly pelagic (living in the open sea), sometimes
seen hundreds of kilometres from land. Live-bearing.

Notes: The most widely distributed of all sea-snakes. The specific name means 'flat-tailed'. **Venomous.**

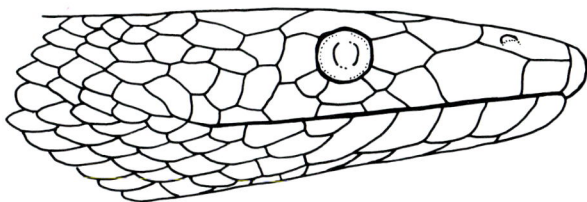

Figure 10 Side of head of Yellow-bellied Sea-snake showing
elongated snout

Recently Extinct Species

Dinosaurs, Mesozoic marine reptiles and other species (such as turtles and pterosaurs) that died out in New Zealand in the distant geological past leaving truly fossilised remains are beyond the scope of this book. However, there are several recently extinct species known from museum specimens or subfossil bones (bones that are hundreds, thousands or a few tens of thousands of years old). Those for which subfossil bones exist probably died out as a result of the ecological disruption caused by the Maori settlement of New Zealand, which began about 1000 years ago. More than 30 species of birds became extinct at the same time.

Aurora Frog
Leiopelma auroraensis   Worthy, 1987

This species is known only from subfossil bones found in Aurora Cave, Lake Te Anau. It was a very robust relative of Hochstetter's Frog (p. 14) and measured about 60 mm SVL.

Markham's Frog
Leiopelma markhami   Worthy, 1987

Subfossil bones of this species, related to Hochstetter's Frog (p. 14), have been found in caves throughout the North and South Islands. It grew to 50–60 mm SVL and is named after

Geoffrey Markham, who pioneered the study of subfossil frog bones in New Zealand.

Waitomo Frog
Leiopelma waitomoensis   Worthy, 1987

This species is known as a subfossil from cave deposits throughout the North Island, with most material having come from the Waitomo district. It was the largest *Leiopelma* (up to about 100 mm SVL) and a close relative of Archey's and Hamilton's Frogs (pp. 11 and 13).

Kawekaweau
Hoplodactylus delcourti   Bauer & Russell, 1986

This is by far the largest of all geckos (370 mm SVL) and is known from just one mounted specimen, without collection data, at the Natural History Museum in Marseille, France. Its placement in the genus *Hoplodactylus* means it most probably came from New Zealand. It could be the kawekaweau of Maori

Kawekaweau   *Hoplodactylus delcourti*

legend. The specimen has a yellowish-brown back with dark reddish-brown longitudinal stripes. Named after Alain Delcourt of the Marseille Museum, who first recognised the significance of the specimen.

Northland Skink
Cyclodina northlandi   Worthy, 1991

Subfossil bones of this species have been found in caves near Kaeo and Waipu in Northland. It was the largest New Zealand skink (at least 160–170 mm SVL).

Narrow-bodied Skink
Oligosoma gracilicorpus   (Hardy, 1977)

Described from one faded museum specimen (97 mm SVL) collected in the Hokianga area before 1955. No other specimens have come to light and nothing is known of its distribution and habits.

Further Reading

More information on New Zealand's frogs and reptiles may be found in the following publications:

Barnett, S. 1985. *New Zealand in the Wild. An Illustrated A-Z of Native and Introduced Birds, Mammals, Reptiles and Amphibians*. Collins (Auckland).

Gill, B.J. 1986. *Collins Handguide to the Frogs and Reptiles of New Zealand*. Collins (Auckland).

Newman, D.G. (editor) 1982. *New Zealand Herpetology. New Zealand Wildlife Service Occasional Publication No. 2* (Wellington).

Newman, D. 1987. *Tuatara*. John McIndoe (Dunedin).

Newman, D.G. (editor) 1994. *Special Issue: Second World Congress of Herpetology*. New Zealand Journal of Zoology 21(4): 317–490 (Wellington).

Pickard, C.R. & Towns, D.R. 1988. *Atlas of the Amphibians and Reptiles of New Zealand. Conservation Sciences Publication No. 1* (Wellington).

Robb, J. 1977. *The Tuatara*. Meadowfield (Shildon, UK).

Robb, J. 1986. *New Zealand Amphibians and Reptiles in Colour.* Revised ed. Collins (Auckland).

Sharell, R. 1975. *The Tuatara, Lizards and Frogs of New Zealand*. Collins (Auckland).

Towns, D.R. 1988. *A Field Guide to the Lizards of New Zealand.* 2nd edition. *New Zealand Wildlife Service Occasional Publication No. 7* (Wellington).

Whitaker, A.H. & Thomas, B. 1989. *New Zealand Lizards: an Annotated Bibliography*. DSIR (Lower Hutt).

Photography credits

Photographs by Tony Whitaker except for:

George Balazs — *Dermochelys coriacea, Chelonia mydas, Lepidochelys olivacea*

Alison Cree — *Leiopelma archeyi, Sphenodon guntheri*

Brian Enting — *Oligosoma infrapunctatum*

Rod Morris — *Leiopelma hochstetteri, Cyclodina whitakeri, Caretta caretta*

Richard Parrish — *Oligosoma fallai*

Paddy Ryan — *Pelamis platurus*

Marcus Simons — *Oligosoma notosaurus*

Bruce Thomas — *Leiopelma hamiltoni, Hoplodactylus delcourti, H. granulatus, H. nebulosus, H. stephensi, Naultinus manukanus, N. tuberculatus, Oligosoma lineoocellatum, O. stenotis, Oligosoma* sp.

Index